The Fiesta

By the same author

Poems
Angles and Circles
Sad Grave of an Imperial Mongoose
Penguin Modern Poets 23 (with Edwin Muir and Adrian Stokes)
Discoveries of Bones and Stones
Ingestion of Ice Cream
A Skull in Salop
Collected Poems
The Isles of Scilly
Under the Cliff
Several Observations

Anthologies
Faber Book of Epigrams and Epitaphs
The Penguin Book of Ballads
Faber Book of Love Poems
Faber Book of Popular Verse
Rainbows, Fleas and Flowers
Faber Book of Nonsense Verse

Celebration and Criticism
The Goddess of Loving
Britain Observed
The Englishman's Flora
The Contrary View
Notes from an Odd Country
Poems and Poets

The Fiesta
and Other Poems

Geoffrey Grigson

Secker & Warburg · London

First published in England 1978 by
Martin Secker & Warburg Limited
54 Poland Street, London W1V 3DF

Copyright © Geoffrey Grigson 1978

436 18840 6

Printed in Great Britain by
REDWOOD BURN LIMITED
Trowbridge & Esher

For H.M.J.G.

By what influence
Do the new leaves come out
On the poplars in the dry barranco
After the winter drought?

Acknowledgments

Poems in this volume have first appeared in the *Listener*, the *New Statesman*, *Encounter*, the *London Magazine*, *Country Life* and *Poetry* (Chicago).

Contents

The High Castle

Set on their rondures rise,
Rise into the blue air, from most
Green slopes of grass, tapering
White paper towers. And never

In the well-shed turned now
Is the great wooden windlass
Of the most deep well. Here
Guides and parties only

Come and go. All now, all houses,
Are a depth below. And bridges,
Crossing a lake of river down
Below. Down, down there are

Lorries, affairs, vines, broccoli,
And flowers. And you two walk in
This unreal blue, on this unreal
Grass, circling the white towers.

Saumur

Driving through dead Elms

Elms have died, over a green land
Is each, here, there, a leafless sad
Black upright drawing. It is
Winter in summer.

Through each delicate dead drawing
Sky shows. In some are black
Nests. But no rooks are in and out about
New life cawing

Before leaves are coming. Why must that
Which is all the time here, be now
Visible — the winter,
Winter in summer?

Visit from a Biographer

Someone I do not know today comes,
Dear Norman, from God knows where
In great America, to ask about your
Days in life. Today is grey,
A Sunday three weeks or so from yet one more,
One more Christmas Day. And it rains,
And a toad-house frowns, up our one
Road, a puzzled face. Squared eyes, a most
Red mouth. A facial fungus. With no neck,
And on the ground is it a parody of life.

This stranger: Am I to tell him where
You cut your name in the now
Fallen chalk? Am I to say
Whose silk stockings shared your top
Lefthand drawer? Steady the rain.
My newly washed white hair is wild.
A stir makes the gate creak.
Am I to say for whom, or why,
You wrote *Shepherdess*,
Show me now where I may sleep?

To Ivor Gurney

Wind-driven falling water flashed,
A blue passed, birds turned,
Wind made a growl and threshed.

It went through you, you flashed,
You were the blue, you turned,
You were the air,

Separate in a double-glazed
Kind cruel delusive false
Climate here. Your book

Of ecstasy I have picked up. It is
On my knee, at the moment it supports
My paper, and what I write, and me.

Hare and Burke

Maybe it is tragedy that possibilities of being
Fall short of exaltation of thinking
And exquisiteness and tenderness of feeling.
Still, the one is the condition of the others.

How I detest those antics of Hare,
His wagging ears, his fool's face and
His advancing teeth, capering above graves
As if there were no thinking, no feeling,

Only being; those antics also
Of Burke, black-chinned, sullen
In his open shirt, lurking in lecture-rooms
And in the dulled heads of the insecure,

Complaining that he is not loved,
Exhuming to denigrate and smear
Adipocere, and poison of his own personal
Chemicals, upon being; pontificating

On our times as if the phrase *Under
The greenwood tree* had not been devised
In despite of dying, in times of terror. As
Pasternak and Akhmatova understood.

Joan of Arc's Stone, Le Crotoy

Estuary without glory. Brown waters,
Plural waters, plural loops
Of more pallid intersecting selvedges
Advance, hiss, and cover shine
Of mud and lap a fisherman's leaning

Black boat, surround it, and advance,
As brown as clouds. And clouds as brown
As advancing waters smudge
The supposed clemency of what we name
Heaven, in slow bars.

They wait, for the turn. Then cross
These flats with her — one or two
Birds lift — and set her rubicund
Chilled face to being
Judged, and fire.

*

Lay any flowers, sea lavender,
Mesembrianthemum, under the
Grey stone which tells you this.

Ones divided from Evil

Homewards; having driven someone who came
To interview me back to the station. Poets, I now reflect,
As the sun Helios, Apollo, All-revealer by light,
Goes down in an autumn display of gilding, should

Refuse to be interviewed. They enunciate follies,
Slipshod. Then afterwards they think, naturally, of right
Things to have said. But I admit some questions of his now
Stir me to emotion. Helios has gone, and my

Emotion of man is that temples and gods were inside,
Through all our long time of unknowing; that as well
The best of our gods, and their temples,
For instance, that one in the brightest denying

Of storm or dismay on the top of Aegina, were better
Than a god might have expected, with reason,
Of his creators. Our measure is how much worse
Might have been our so imperfect unknowing creations.

Scent pinched from thyme. And always evil a Nixon
Or Childeric. Those evil who crash lids of their
Treasure on to evil hands of their children. And the scent
Of herbs and, after all correcting, of ones divided from evil.

Morning of Zero

Looking out of the window
Through the soul of man
I see Zero smoothing the whole world
With a white hand.
Light is also white at the back of the hills:
When the sun clears them
It will loosen the white hand,
Roofs will darken and will steam,
Grass will become green,
But it will not much warm the land.

First Visit, 10.15

She was infamous, for great
Lovers in her day.
How her *château* has now
Outside and inside as well
Become stained and grey.
On panels the delicate paint flakes away.

From April Fool's Day to
October we pay
To see her curtained curved
Corner bed in which
We may suppose they lay,
Looking as if we cared what the guide has to say.

But how all spirit of loving,
Or of living, has crumbled away.
How the crown of this old
Creature ahead of me shows
Bald through her grey.
Coins tinkle, we queue out into day.

There's a breeze: it is just
Sufficient to sway
Clematis flowers, white ones,
And pink ones, hanging from a slender
Iron arch in front of the grey,
And about these the guides have not a thing to say.

18

The Fiesta:
Homines Ludentes atque Precantes

Geranium men pull through a high
Village carts which are pink and red
With petals of geranium. Spokes,
Rims, hubs, men, are petalled with
Geranium. So this over-the-ocean
Village plays, by custom and by rule,
And candles elsewhere today are set
In hollows of cathedrals on their
Iron trays and women pray, not all
Because they are old or mad. Between
These flowers, these shawled women
Who pray, these twinkling lights,
Questions I ask again. Time
Have we taken out of pilgrimage,
Difference have we deep-frozen
Out of seasons, darkness we have
Diluted, and have darkened day; and it is
Clear to me that now I shall never
Walk dusty and burnt, by day
Noticing the yellow poppies and black
Cranesbill and flowers of dampness
As blue as day, at night led by
The Milky Way; shall never
At last in the soft rain enter
That granite shrine, of that saint
Whose presence ever in Spain
Is fiction certainly.

        Once in Norfolk, home
Of my ancestors, pulling to one
Side, I let a procession go by, singing,
Self-consciously bearing a Good
Friday cross to what there is left, which
Is not much, since level with
The ground do lie those towers

Which with their golden glittering
Tops did pierce out to the sky,
Of the shrine of the Lady of Walsingham
About which Erasmus was scornful.
Did I envy them? But then making
A god out of the non-entity of gods,
Recognizing necessity, and rejecting
As If, tell me, my being, now,
What shall I do? Or what shall maintain
My being? Give me an answer. Is
It enough, willing myself to play
By my rules, and to pray by
My ritual, that is to reiterate
Hope, since no *deus* descends
Ex machina? Enough to be called by
All shall be better, by *At last*
Shall none be exploited? And out
Of the indignity of a knowing and
Worried animal being beckoned
In that way?
       Well, that would be something.
Saints to be sure I admire, thinking
In deserts, burnt by salt upon
Rocks circled by whales, licked
Warm by otters, cherishing swallows
Returned, visited by dreamers, even
By the exceedingly bad; or made
Wonderful in glass which is
The colour of poppies and cornflowers
And sticks of angelica. But
Excuse me if I maintain there are
Saints not superior to the secular
Martyrs of hope, or shall I say
To St. Morris, William, of
Doves upon blue and of the blown
Willows of Kelmscott. What vision,
What moment of happiness in the procession

Of moments is expressed by the carts
And men with geranium scented and
Petalled, on this mountain over clouds, over
An ocean?

Aphrodite
(from the Greek)

Queen of this beach, here by
   The swell of the sea
I have a house which is simple
   Yet pleasant to me.

I delight in this wide
   Terrible sea,
I delight in your prayers for
   Aid from me.

Give me my due, then a breeze
   Will flow fair from me,
And help you, in love,
   And over the sea.

Young Death

And now it is the longest night,
And I am awake thinking of him
In this St Lucy's night.

How no fine-fingered hand sleepily
Moves into the slack of his side.
How he wakes up

And their full bed is empty. How
It is not true. How — lorries begin —
After all, after all, no

Body shifts by him warmly
In their bed. No one is there
who can be comforted.

Reflections on a Bright Morning

You are dead. So again and again
I return to contemplate this abominable
Brevity of living. How is it so
Loving and exhilarating, so always

Eager a chieftain of living should be
Living no more? It isn't enough
To say, Your perceptions remain; it isn't
Enough to read them, alone, out loud,

And to love them, and to remember you.
Whose investigating presence, brilliant
By day, hovered on shivering extremest
Wings over the night flowers of perfume:

You are not living. There is no you
To whom it can be something
That we live in part by your perceiving,
And praise you. And there, speak

With what resignation we may,
Is the distress. Remain mornings, middays,
Evenings, nights, and men's most curious
Coruscations. But, you are not living.

24

To Hermes
(from the Greek)

Wayside Hermes, this share of a fine
    Bunch of grapes, this piece
Of lardy cake out of the oven, a black
    Fig, an olive soft on the gums,
These slicings of a round cheese, some
    Cretan corn, a heap of fine ground
Meal, then this concluding cup of wine
    I dedicate to you. Allow the
Cyprian, my goddess, to enjoy them too.
    And I will, I promise, offer
On the pebbly shore a white-
    Footed kid to the pair of you.

Was Yeats a Fascist?

For ever the wild heart sings,
For ever they argue and they act the fool,
For ever at Coole his wild swans rise
And beat their wings.

Neither Here nor There

This is what he told me on the phone
Of the old poet, very long single
Hairs curling out of his chin, missed
From the bar, in the interval of his

Upstairs poetry reading: he was found
In the Gents peeing into his pint of beer
And muttering How awful these lefties
Are. And his young lefty admirers

Felt they were seeing life,
And touching the peculiarities
Of art, and surrounded him, and with
Embarrassment hustled him away in a taxi.

Funeral

I dreamt you were dead and your grace
Now was gone for ever,
And I was not there to love you,
Nor was your lover.

I sent a cable to your handsome
Feckless old father.
I could not remember the name
Or address of your lover.

There was no sign around of
Your husband either. So in me
I buried you, in a corner, and there was
No other mourner.

The Mynah

Is it the duty of visitors to this
bird garden
to admire Beauty?

> *Meeow wow-wow* replies the Mynah
> inclining his head. Other birds
> in this rusty bird garden I
> neglect. I listen to him
> instead.

Is it the duty of visitors to this
bird garden
to admire Beauty?

> Macaws gallop raggedly
> overhead, their bellies are red,
> *meeow wow-wow* this sad ape-bird
> for the tenth time says. I
> attend to him instead.

Is it my duty in this unsacred
garden of birds
to admire Beauty?

> This noodle wags flaps of yellow
> at the back of his head,
> and simulates a cat, then a poodle's
> yap. And I like that, I
> talk to him instead.

And though we may suppose
it is a duty in a bird garden
to admire Beauty,

and though pinker than usual in the last
sun shrimp-pink flamingoes stand
on one pin leg, what I wait
for is an eleventh sad, mad
meeow wow-wow from that cocked head.

Silly bugger, says the Mynah,
Silly bugger, instead.

Piptete ton Obolon

Outside I admire, its foot ringed
With stones, a great leaning old
Olive tree fluffed with the two-
Toned yellow cream of its flowers, then
I open as far as I can the shrivelled
Doors, south, north and west, three
Sets of doors, to entice light enough
To photo in colour St Francis,
In a faint fresco, with the birds. But
Not light enough moves the black bar,
And I notice over a box a scrawl
Which says *Piptete ton obolon.*
The word *obolon*, I reflect, has no ring
Of April. Louis's poem I remember
And the hard black varicose veins
Of Charon. *Piptete ton obolon.*
It rattles into the box. Outside
And below blue heights and blue hollows
Recur, and daintily from a stone
Fountain water trickles away
Under fig trees, passes the sloping
Olive, reaches a gnarled *Liquidambar*
Orientalis, aromatic feeder of larvae
Of elegant moths, then goes to ground
Among flowers. One flower protrudes
From a spathe a black prick like
The prick of a dog, and it stinks. Yet
How elegantly curved is this black prick
Of a dog; how splendidly disposed
Inside on the green spathe from which
It emerges, are also the spots of
Ultimate black — if you take my meaning
Regarding, and disregarding, the coin,

Such being the elegiac deliciousness
Of season and place, of sunlight, of trees
And of flowers, of this small church
Here by itself, and its faded frescoes
Inside, and of you shaping all this in delight.

West Window

Consolations were: Christ, Heaven,
Judgement, devils at the mouth
Of great Leviathan, glow of these
Through minds stained with the bright
Salts of cobalt, copper, iron. *And now —*
What now, whispers to himself upon
His knees the priest, *now time hurts me,*
Home walks away, and deserts me,
And everything is beast?

His Swans

Remote music of his swans, their long
Necks ahead of them, slow
Beating of their wings, in unison,
Traversing serene
Grey wide blended horizontals
Of endless sea and sky.

Their choral song: heard sadly, but not
Sad: they sing with solemnity, yet cheerfully,
Contentedly, though one by one
They die.
One by one his white birds
Falter, and fall, out of the sky.

The Return

Summering mild-voiced birds have gone away,
In locked gardens are now leaves no more
Than moved by a small secret shifting.
Edges behind are smudged blue-grey of

A changing season. Under cliffs, under
The promenade's wild wiry tamarisks slow
Machines do not each morning early comb
The smart beaches clear of oil. Now

Grey and obese snakes in these locked
Gardens have again taken to sleeping
By the unentered doors below the continuing
Morning Glory slightly swaying flowers.

For it is ten days since cars, heavy with
Brown young and strapped-on, last-minute
Packages, sneaked home to their far off
Neighbourhoods of flats and factories.

Seville

Strangers only come to this strange
City by the routes of air. Then skirt
Forked olive trees in red earth speedily,
Then ragged factories.

A great cathedral. Let it be, the canon said,
So big they'll think us mad. Gold
Leaf of the Indies glitters up
To vaults of gloom.

The Discoverer's great black catafalque,
On great black shoulders in this gloom.
God must be buried here, he cannot live
In this great gloom.

Great heat relents outside. *Murderers,*
Guardia Civilia, Assassins, declare
Half whitened words across a perfect wall,
Blood of a bull — and

All crush round — reddens a T.V.
Screen. Needles of crystal water rise, Becquer's
Three girls in crinolines of marble swoon
Around their tree,

Astarte's doves, white doves, from palms
Flow down. This is, round parks, the city
Of Peru. Through trees a thin black priest
Extrudes his holy hands.

Then clouded flowers of jalapa, when dark
Descends and dancing sounds, are white
And frilled with pink and are at
Midnight most perfumed.

Epitaph

They buried me without
A penny for my fare,
So how long do I have
To hang round here
On this dank gapped
Wharf under this
Mud-reflecting sky,
Watching the polluted
Stream go by?

Musician with Green Wings

In that mouchette, too much aloft for poles
To smash and tinkle down, — listen!
In that high window, in that mouchette,
In a dulled, dark, damp church,

His green wings fining to a point
Over his head, on a red ground, one
Angel music-maker, floating,
Making on his long instrument

Such music as would later grand
Teutons between ages draw from
The possibilities of sound. On that
Damp side, faded Ecclesia

Triumphs. On this, faded blind Synagogue
Bends her deject, defeated head.
Dreams. This saffron music-maker
Is playing dreams of the dead times.

Hellas

If I say I have come at last home
And here marble is warm
And these shrubs are pink by the
Coarser rocks and shake by the sea.

If I say I have come home
And here walls are whiter
Than paper and here at last I see
How red wine does apply to a sea.

If I say I have come back
To the starting and here
White high boats lay slow
Magnificent breasts on the sea —

I have to admit to me, like all
Other homes, this home-as-before
Cannot longer, and as well
Warmly, be home around me.

Golden Find of a Small
Clay Figure

Would it be, Goddess of Loving, since
Your clay cooled, say five thousand plus
Or minus a few hundred years?

Then the god-maker fixed this bead of
New gold into your belly-hole and these two
Gold rings in your ears.

The Great Headland

Who croaks Decay for all?
Who offers the Dove?
In the cliff-egg life spins,
And does not fall.

Colonels and Judges

Under oil lamps of evensong
God lifted up his face
And proclaimed a twisted blessing
On the twisted human race.

He was their invention who
Have invented worse,
Letting colonels set commandoes
Round their crumbling church.

The congregation leaves,
Guns titter round the graves
And those who are not corpses
Now again are slaves.

But now observe the colonels
On a waterless isle,
Shirtless and unshaven
And awaiting trial.

And observe the judges
Who've turned their coats again
To uphold with anxious
Virtue laws of God and men.

A Love Letter

Eurydice,
        A short retrospective and also
Prospective love letter. I have been reading
A critic of the plastic arts and I decide that like
The works of Ed Moses of California you are
"An idiosyncratic composite of tissue,
Nylon, and rohplex", which — now wait
For it — "is delicately and seductively
Tactile". And I thought — now, why was that? —
Of the goddess well-oiled (don't misunderstand
Me) arriving (on the way she had
Noticed with satisfaction the coupling
Of cat-a-mountains) to bed with Anchises
In his shepherding hut on Mount Ida.
Believe me, what an idiosyncratic compound
He found her, most delicately, and seductively,
Tactile, as she encouraged him to unhook
Her golden adornments, from Asprey's. Had she
The quality also of "seeming tenuous while
Being substantial"? Of course. Like yourself,
Eurydice. And did Anchises exhibit a continuing
"Predilection for discreet, hesitant effects, for
A complexity of quiet incidents"? The hesitancy
Was not hers, the subtlety was hers entirely.
But having this subtlest and most able instructor
He learned quickly. And on herself no
"Desiccated texture was exposed, or painted
Out in a pale colour". Also "dextrous execution
Kept the activity close to the surface". But
Inside deeply, as well. "Seductive material
And subtle effects." But on a real and not
"An abstract environmental and kinetic field",
On which, when the kinetics were over, well-

Oiled Aphrodite turned over, though tender,
To sleep, within a few minutes actually (you
Know what I mean, Eurydice) snoring. O amore,
Amore. Though enclosed in a perfume which isn't
Exhaled at all by the works of Ed Moses.

Chaire.

On Not Learning Russian

Peculiar Alphabet, you lay, in
My dream, widely, letting me in,
Conferring on me your unfamiliar
Shapes, your sounds also,
For the sake of him.

But it is too late. I look
Through your great railings.
Your avenue. Leading in glitter
To your palaces of more brilliant
Yellow and blue.

I cannot pick the great lock.
Now, Cold Alphabet, snow falls.
Too late for me to begin,
Too late to attempt to come in,
Even for him.

Halving of a Pear

An item of best being is
Halving this pear and in its
Ivory seeing this black
Star of seeds.

Also pointing this black
Star in ivory out to you,
And you agreeing, is
An item of best being.

The Fisherman

"Natives of the place"
Continue to walk in hard
Hide shoes with pointed ends. Increased
In width by ten, what was the strolling track
Of goats, kids, women, children
And men, is black and hard
Sunshine remains twelve hours per day
In which wide glare a distantly big
Factory shows in space cleared
Of fossiliferous scratching
Rocks and delicately curving
Wild magenta flowers.

More must be fed, a new
Slaughter-house occupies a limestone edge.
More blood than in days of
Sacrificing flows. More blood
Flows down; out, into sea of blue,
Crimsoning an arc.
A man who does not work today
Fishes in the crimsoned arc, he holds
A white carnation in his lips
And sucks the stem.

Harsh the glare is from mid-morning
To mid-afternoon. The hooter goes,
But not for sleep. A good globe
Our Earth was
For living as we can.
Most that is wrong with our good
Globe was always man. I become with age,
The poet of wonder in his letter says, more
Charitable, and all the time the more
Contemptuous of man.

Find in Hupei

Two millennia, two thousand
And one hundred years ago, and rather more,
You died, Han Emperor's servant of the middle rank,
And they embalmed you.

Now they've found you, in red liquor, in
Your tomb. And all your joints move supply still, if
They are moved,
And still you are dead. Your servants wrote

Your name on a jade seal, and slipped it
In your mouth. They gave you sticks of ink and a reed
Pen and real food too, dates, ginger in a bamboo box
And fish and pork. They gave you clothes as well.

But miniature and carved of wood
Your horses of the wind, low water-buffalo, and
Boats and chariots surrounding you.
Inside themselves your servants knew that dead

Was dead. You would not live again. Or speak that
Name. Perhaps. But no, but no. You would
Not live again. And are dead still, and I
Say still for you, for me, Poor man! Poor man!

Deity not Deified

He would have lived, if they had cut him clear
Of that rock, if they had uttered the word
Over him, then sledded him downhill there.

He would have lived if they had pulled him
Up with grass ropes, and set him to stare, from
Shadows of eyes, out to sea, on a platform here.

He would have lived, if they had ever come back,
Ever divided him from the placenta of that
Mindless scarf-catching summit high up there.

In the Ford

As if modes and times remained the same
For ever they are there, a posing
Couple of landscape painters *en plein*
Air, as if they were strong Pissarro

And another, in a river, on their stools,
Their easel legs as well in water,
Below a broken waterwheel, bandanas
Round their heads, painting

Green shades and shapes on
Rippling surfaces. Two amateurs. I would
Not wet my shoes to round their
Elbows and to see what these two

Make of moments of green shapes
And shades. But that was years ago.
Whenever now I pass that ford I slow
And expect to see them stuffed or

Statues there, fixed, intent,
For ever — handing each other borrowed
Eyes, repeating what those grand ones painted
Over and over again. Yet all the same —

Watching Bonelli's Eagles

Bonelli? Was he Zeus?
Of course the bird-book does not
answer and I continue watching
them, thinking that although

"birds of prey" is our phrase
for eagles, they will descend
to eat at times coleoptera
and carrion; in which

they resemble, I say, if not
Zeus, lord of the white
Olympos, certainly ourselves; yet,
like this, to observe a party

of these aviators slowly
and broadly planing above blunt
points of mountain in cool
light (which has not yet

come down to illuminate
the minute black trees), in-
scribing a part of their nature
and cutting without change

of speed into each other's
sunny trajectories,
is suggestive at least of
strength and of measure,

minus pomposity or conceit,
an empyrean example to other
powerful eaters of carrion,
gods, or presidents

of states, or presidents of
multi and again multi-
national corporations, such
as down here we have created.

Occasion in Westminster Abbey

Deck-chairs, in the park,
Are empty. A few
Walk below their umbrellas
Under yellowing trees. Pelicans
By the lake crouch
Pallidly yellow, and wet.
It is, over London, grey.

Inside, now, in the Abbey everything rises
And levels. Gently the frilled boys
Are singing gentlest music by Haydn.
Quid prodest, quid prodest, O mortalis?

Microphones cannot bring to the last
Stalls of the choir of gold
The old actor's voice intoning
"In the prison of his days

Teach the free man how to praise."
And we are blessed now. And I
Am not one to say no to a blessing. And
Now it is over. We tread recognizing

Each other. We pass Dryden to your
Black stone, Rare One, and read on it
For ourselves your lines we scarcely
Could hear. Poets are talking.

One is off, he says, in the morning
To Prague, his manner eager, his hair
Needing a wash, his glasses half out
Of his pocket in a frayed case.

No rain now outside, now
In the park again. No rain.
Instead a blessed low interference
Of sunlight magicking grass
And the yellowing trees,
Rare One, for a while into
Heaven, so that I do not
Care to repeat *Quid prodest, quid*
      Prodest, O mortalis?

Remembering George Barnes, on the
Anniversary of his starting of
the Third Programme

Not given to Scotch eggs and shandy in the pub
But crushing poppadums in your Oriental Club,
Or pacing between B.H. and Harley Street,
Upset, dear George, and sometimes indiscreet,
You showed yourself, whatever you were at,
Never the uncultivated cultural-democrat.
You would have preferred pursuing knowledge,
Presiding over the best-lawned Cambridge college —
A cynic? No. Maybe a compromiser,
By nurture, between the average and the wiser.
For that we had the lip to call you shallow,
Nicknaming you the Pillar of Marshmallow.
But then you saw a condition of the mind to come
Pillared on caryatids of chewing-gum,
And salved your admitted treason to the Word
In that fine Programme so rapidly given the bird.
Ear-counting colleagues jeered at Barnes's Folly
And your ridiculous elitist squandering of lolly
Better dispensed to purchase nastier names
And set up series of more babyish parlour games.
"George will hire the Greek Ambassador to read, in Greek,
All Aristophanes, in ninety-nine instalments, week by week."
Yet for a while evoking the easy sneer,
Fine words, fine notes were waved through the startled air,
For a while the bay-trees in the black tubs glistened,
And even the Muses sent for a radio and listened.

I did not say Content

It's everywhere, and if we are
Its archaeologists and dig, stale
Excrement lies under
Excrement, and further down

Most ancient and compact
Dried excrement; and under that
Lies coprolite, so many thousand
Excremental years B.P., B.C.

Yet here and there, don't get me
Wrong, is sacrament,
Both new and then to all depths
Stratified; of hand which holds

The hand. I did not say,
Sacrament which is priesthood's
Excrement. So, be comforted.
Content I did not say.

Kazanluk

Ourselves surrounding with symbols of living
And of returning to living,

For aeons we have been turning unliving
Away, for aeons charading.

So our young queen, abandoned to living,
Comes to this funeral feasting.

She lays her soft hand on her consort's
Arm, which is discoloured and chilly,

And to him tread the straight girls who carry
Trays of Persephone's symbols,

And the cakes on his table are broken.
Close the tomb up. Those living

Have come out to light. Fit the cut
Stones, heap earth on the mound,

Lash the horses, lean forward. Drive faster
And faster the cars of this furious

Living — your scarves streaming airborne
Behind you — around and around

And around. More faintly
Shrill the thin gold
Trumpets under the ground.

It does not Clear

To be seen, no cliff. Fog only, in which,
A substance, thorn-bushes, on the surface,

Are black shapes. Beyond, above, on either
Side this fog which is not shifting, is

Not moved away. You'd like to see riders
Along the cliff-top, jackdaws

On the up-draught rising?
Comforting; a film excerpt of this ancient

World. You would have these riders of
Which century? Slow,

Not too far to see necks of their horses
Curving, so much sky, so linear

A progression. Cavalry? Hunters?
Killers? Well, simple enjoyers

Of being in the air and young,
Looking ahead, seeing down

Over trees, over an endlessness of
Hamlet-speckled fields.

Even then if there was no fog as there is
Now, would your clear line of riders

Pass; and leave a blank and so destroy your
Earliest wonder of the day.

Crow, Rat, and Toad

To the crow leave the rat,
Refuse your arm to the toad.
Know what you are at,
On the identical road.

Death of Cicero

Slaves, you set down Cicero's litter,
And Cicero stuck out his head,
And with one swish a lieutenant
Struck off his head.

Did you weep,
Slaves, when you saw
Cicero dead,
And that rolling head?

Conversation with a Clerical Father

At times I talk to my dead
Father, I talk to him
About inevitable passing.

   I say, You were young, and then
Your young wife died.
You then, I say, required
The consolation you
Had preached. Years went.
Older, old at last,
Your whiskers fluffed and white,
Your hair behind a greasy
Iron-grey fall, I ask,
Did you take to asking if
In this land of life,
Of things you had hoped
To do, you had managed
Any at all?

   I can't say a mild sun
Warmed you finally.
I see you in the bed
In which you made a love
I'd think which slightly
Puzzled you, reader, by
Calling, of St Paul.
It was the bed in which
Your single daughter
And your sons were born.
And no hand
With particular tenderness
Wiped your great brow,
There was no hand to hold
Your hand. Only your deep
Unconsciousness then filled

The room. No thoughts,
You could not think at all,
About that better land,
My God, *that land*, you had
Heralded to others
Dying in their bed.

   O I do recall
How your broad thumb
Pressed on a short
Fountain-pen whose black
From age had turned grey-
Green. With that shakily
You wrote your words
Of life to me when I
Became twenty-one.

         * * *

Now, lovers, rearers of lovely
Children, yes, and priests,
Enjoy, there being no
Better land. The broad catalpa
Leaves turn brown,
Wrinkle, fall, and clutter
The wet ground.

Watch, while you can,
The November rockets climb,
The fire-wheels turn,
The silver fountains
Lighting naked trees.
And if you like, in being
Thankful — though to whom? —
Sink to an old
Attitude upon your knees.

Biology of Grief

Can I beat myself now for that
Grief? Evergreens do know their
Fall of leaf. In the end griefs

Are complete. Griefs take at first
To hiding away in the cupboard
Where photos of you and me

Fade, I walking under a black
Head of hair, you sweetly breasted
And slim; where — you removed them —

Are stored no photos of her; where —
I turned them out too — are no
Photos of him. We are older. Have

Changed. He and she — and you
Can't remember his name — in
Feature and age stay the same.

Swallow Cave over the Sea

Swallows have lost eaves in which they trusted.
These swallows curve to their grand conch
Where for more centuries than are known
They have nested.

Shark-boats heave by, planes in a vee drone.
Indifferent, uninterrupted, happy, a thousand
Of them, these swallows weave their
Wild summer home.

The Swallows

On a clear wire above a hollow of the air
Sharply these fat young ones strain their wings.
They peck, they trim, they act full-grown,
Then are young ones, quivering, when a parent
Curves from that great hollow of the air
Delivering to them insects on the wing. These
Birds are not aware of time, age, storms, weakness,
Tiredness, which are their enemies. It is we
Who have made up tales of them, they
Live without fear,
Without remembering. And they trust
Less to the hard earth than to the great
Hollow of the air.

The Swallows Returning

An old swallow, weak for returning
Yet compelled to fly,
He joins the young. They are strong
And stretch and preen, and are

Chattering eagerly. Around
Are favoured alleys and valleys
Of the air between elm trees,
Ledges, their dipping

Surfaces, known premises. Now,
Do they all lift and fly,
For now it is time finally
To leave all these.

Pure Red

Lifting my face, eyes shut,
   To a lifting sun,
I consider this morning is
   Elementally and well begun.

In front of my closed eyes
   A situation of pure red
Floats, flickered with genuine
   Gold, till I turn my head

And mottles of purple
   And dull blue intervene
Which re-colour themselves to
   Suffusions of a blotched green.

These are not pleasant, so
   I turn back my head
And regain that elementality
   Of a most pure red.

A Bright Decay

This side of the window glass
A bending stem holds up
A weakening flower.
How do I say

The red colour of a weakening flower?

Outside the window glass,
The late snow falling, the falling
Hypnotizing snow, the falling
Falling snow, this side

The red colour of a weakening flower?

Return

To the sea always this path goes.
The land dips,
Steeply this path crooks
Pocked dribbling rocks,
Upright on which such succulent
Pennywort grows.
Lower, to the sea
Corkscrewing, lower, lower,
This path goes.

    Always to a free
    Infinity, beyond
    The cut for wagons, the water-
    Fall, sand-sunk stream,
    And cowries,
    The path goes.

       *

Always from the sea, back,
Rounding rocks, under
Black bent roofs
Of thorn, over
Worn slab stiles below
Wild sycamores, back, back, back
This rough path climbs, into
At last on top
This gracious alley, raked,

And precise, of limes.
Here's the white
Gate,
Gravel, and the short,
Fern-green
Superseded tower.

                *

Obvious the gravestones,
The parked car. It's late.
Say what you mean, I interpret
This lonely creak of the gate.
By the quaint, O quaint shot
Smuggler's stone *Know what
You are*, I interpret
The urging of a yet visible one white
Not obsequious foreign flower.

Mosaic at Torcello

God's not to blame for God.
  But hell is hell,
Though God's cable goes
  Wriggling down this

Glitter-wall with voltage
  From his high seat
To start the flame. For that
  Are we to blame.

For God as well. God, have you
  Stopped judging? Now,
Robes off, do you wear
  The pit-rescuer's stinking

Gear, to save those twisters
  In the flame, who
Will not, rightly, scream
  Out your name?

If You had elected to stay

I write — but the letter never is posted — "As I
Dream of you, do you dream of me ever?" Awake, I now
Piece together one supple dream of you. Listen,
Your hairbrush is rasping your hair. Then the scent
Of your still night-dressed body passes, and then comes near
And I say "Oh, if you had elected to stay, had
Elected to stay" — liking that form of my words —
As if it were not all those twenty-three years
Gone by, as if it were yesterday. And as if there was not
A concluding null summer fog outside under which
On the dull concrete the sneaking and stopping small
Lizards are grey.

Bright Piece out of a Dead Sea

i

A sea of dirt, made chemical, of grey
Small waves below which not many fishes
Play, which not a dolphin breaks.
And where it comes to shore frogmen of
Archaics tack a rope to her. Seventeen
Centuries she has passed in water-twilight
Here. Saints — that was our fathers'
Name for them — clapped when Greeks stole
Gold laces from her neck, then, I admit,
Not dragging her sweet backside over her
Stony temenos or bruising her sweet fixed
Smile, carried her to the edge with care
And pitched her from this highest cape
At last, into her sea then blue.

ii

Give her a black pedestal in the best
Museum room. Publish her postcard. Establish
White doves in a cote outside. A television
Eye will see if you begin to pencil
Your name with your girl's name across her
Formerly pink thigh. But observe: most
Days this dead museum is shut. Her white
Doves have become grey. The Graces do
Not attend. She cannot dance with them.
And now she has not a thing to say.

A White Dove

Bedclothes heaped up
Shaped the bare feet, the draped
Legs, draped thighs of a statue
In my room. She was

The state of being young, or not
Too old for expectation, then
Surprise. Missing were this
Statue's upper nakedness

And the famous
Glance of her eyes. I dressed,
I watched this seated
Fragment of the white

Deity of regretted love. I thought,
Let there fly in, the window's
Open, and to her knees now
Flutter a white dove.

Thanks, after a Party

I reflect on the evening before being
Seventy on the pleasures of not
Having met some who have been,
I deduce, sycophantic suppressors.

And on the pleasure of having
In the past sat on the lawn
At the feet of some who have
Greatly deserved our love,

And on the pleasures of having
Experienced epiphanies, not of
Divinity, but of endowments and benisons
Which are for us all.

And if this spring I have stepped
At last up the foot-burnished
Hill of Athene, for that too
I am grateful. Even although

I could, to be sure, like Yeats,
Complain I am one who might
Have had, to begin with, more
Of the love of women, yet

Excited I have been and contented
And soothed by that
At last which came grandly
My way; though with my own

Power of return I have been
Less contented. I who sucked
Honey out of the anthered magenta
Flowers of the fuchsia, have

Seen with surprise today
Features of my long dead in
The gathered living, with pleasure
Observed on mouths which

Tonight will sleepily kiss, again
That strangely continuing
Sweetness which shall, with
Consciousness, grow into kindness.

Death of a Farmyard

Worn out were the buildings, I
Tell you. Worn out. Do you know how
Buildings wear out? Elm walls were
Worm-bored and warped. Rain

Through the gap. Hard stemmed
Wide weeds in the track. Door hinges
Rusted, dropped out. In the lew, strapped
War-wounded Jim wove ropes out of

Hay. Smell of old hay. High
Nettles. Elders. Staddles, no, did
Not keep out rats. String-
Tailed quick feet, rats nipped

Into sacks. And believe it or not,
Two geese were dead and were dry,
Sitting down white around hollow,
Alongside low sties collapsed.

Pulled away, I tell you, all
Pulled away. No yard, no broken
Hay. No Jim. A new house. A new day.
That muck. All pulled away.

Corner of Somehow

I doubt the good of it,
But no one prays,
And if I say that where,
Into this hanger,

This grey mead cuts,
Below nuttal trees and silver
Legs of ash, where
A green cress flows,

Is a corner which is
Holy, I must mean
It is — somehow — deeply
Apt to man. "Somehow",

I must say as well, was once
The god by another name.
"Somehow" was his unspoken
Name; and to him

In these days, I say
Again, and doubt
The good of this, now
No one, no one prays.

Craft Centre, in a derelict Mill

Regarding a blue punt drawn in, stillness
Of a secretive river, sparseness of uneven
Grass half cut, white and blue petunias
Bending from dry pots along a river wall
And amateur arts inserted in the decay of this
Corn mill, and over all to their
Crests huge river trees under a viciously
Hot damp wind swaying whitely — regarding
This, it's old Pissarro, bearded, who does now
Recur to me, since that which I regard, if
He had seen it (this corn mill then lively
With wheel noises, waters, stones revolving
And white dust of flour), now reproduced
In colour catalogues, or hanging in some dollar-
Tax-avoidance gallery, or waiting, humbly,
At a grand auctioneer's, would arrest or
Would invent summer perfection
Of this scene, the old lyricist's strokes
Of paint absorbing tattiness of unhappy
Grass and all ungrace, again. Whereas
In this, uncomfortably, I see impermanence
Not able quietly to be at ease. Again.
    Beyond this thin dry grass with weeds
A white wall has been broken through,
Leaving jagg'd edges; a wide warehouse
Roof removed. Cars are parked there, visitors
Crunch new gravel back to them, clasping
Their wrapped August purchases.

    Also, Pissarro, I have beyond these cars
Lined up, these sad studios, seen, neglected,
Away, out of time active, from the crunched
Gravel — stared into it — a white-stone

Well-head here. Some slates have gone from
Its conical black roof. Down five feet
Dangle inside, over black water, in a green
Circle, long hartstongue ferns, in a cool. These
Grow. These cannot be disturbed by a wind.
These are beyond the reach of hands. Are real.
Painted by you.

Significance of Frail

I learn significance of frail:
Being happy, and not happy, do exist.
And then tomorrow, and some accident.
Some failing. Some collapse of cells.

Then goes that frame in which
Being happy and not happy, anxious,
In little or great pain, subsist,
That which is frail being not

Pallid shell fragments fallen
Among fallen late June
Flowers, being arrangement
Which creates significance. And sensible

Were we at least to say
To frailty *No — too soon.* To ring
(If not grand bells in strong-
Frail towers, if not to swing and ring

Bells dividing time, glad bells, slow
Bells, bells single, saddening,
Apotropaic bells) at least our
Wind-bells hung in trees.

The Man from Byzantium

It was all very well for that royal
English saint to be martyred, they say,
On this shrill Cotswold hill. These monks

Say he picked up his head. Unoriginal.
It was all very well to erect that
Minster over the grass where he fell,

Too narrow, too dark, and too tall.
And here rain also for ever fell; and
The man from Byzantium purchasing wool

Blew his fingers, thinking of eating
His oysters again on the Lampsakene
Shore and seeing the glitter of sun

Run over the gold-leaf screen. He would
Be again at the centre of men, not
Knowing who ruled in the Land of the

Painted or in Chung Kuo. Not
Foreseeing either the Crescent and Star,
Or Old Glory, or Hammer and Sickle,

Or that Byzantium centuries ahead
Should be only the thought of a poem
Written by passion, which saw, in a green

Land even wetter and rougher, revolving
Cycles of time; where the myths were
Halted at least for a while, or

Paused for a while by the grim edge
Of the whale-furrowed floods of — before
Long — an oil-sickened sea.

Extinction

Thinking of your extinction,
I fear my own.
You were rock,
I am a loose stone.

A stone falls
And is reduced to sand.
Yet rock, stone and
Sand are parts of the land.

Issa

Seven syllables —
Busy on them
Till they contained him,
And confessed
Nature at work
In the one moment
When
It seemed at rest.

Birth of Criticism

Larking down the alleys, riled,
Where they are cluttered and defiled
I met a little squalid child

Perusing poems upside down
With a slightly petulant frown
Inside the very squalid town.

Squalid Lamb, I dared to utter,
Native of this mental gutter,
Thrilling to tell marge from butter,

What's reduced you to this pass,
Who should be gambolling on the grass?
Piss off, the Lamb said, Kiss my arse.

I'm reading — — and — — — —
And other masters of cold gravy
And *Imagistes from Tyne to Tavy,*

And my glittering Ph.D.
Will very soon enable me
To climb the professorial tree

And promulgate in flat reviews
Exactly who's who with the Muse
Of Forces, Fields and Avenues.

I gave a teeny cautious cough,
Again the Lamb exclaimed Piss off,
Piss off, you rotten *Sonnen*-toff.

And pissing off I said God damn,
How quickly does the squalid Lamb
Become the bullying pert I Am.

New Literary Memoirs

My goodness, they're already starting to remember!
I thought they weren't three decades old, but now
They're fifty. Some are bald. Some launch bad breath
Across club luncheon tables, fixing labels,
Some teach. Some write bad lead reviews each week.
Some nest inside the littlest little magazines,
As ever. And only yesterday the whole platoon
Appeared (but not to me) so clever.
Now knowing publishers are paying them to say
How — once — they saw George Orwell sporting in the hay,
Or some sly poetaster's wife caught in death's family way.

Respite

Thinking of unhappiness and marriages
I sat on my unmade bed, looked out,
And with surprise, wind having calmed,
Saw Buddha's great face rounded
In our trees. And back came
The wind, and broke the leaves.

The Gull

I acknowledge you showed me the gull.
I see the gull with a shudder. It does
Slip this way and that way, and the sky is
Otherwise void, and the sky and the sea

Do go on to meet, and this white gull
Does go on and waver, and it does become
Smaller, smaller. And I look away. I
Cannot look at you.

Kingdom Come

Old men are glum
Not — or not only —
At the approach
(To them) of what
We once called
Kingdom Come.
They're glum
Because they've learnt
At last, they think,
How that bad-breathed
Fly-eating mongol
Child of Man
The whole while
Shuffles round and
Sucks its thumb.
O Kingdom Come.

Sicut Omnes

I visit my abandoned caves, white dust lies
On what is infrequently disturbed;
On forgotten books and old unbalanced
Accounts. In cavern stables rotten harness
Hangs out of the rock-cut mangers, and I come across
Tools, and weapons, whose handles of hickory crumble
The moment I touch them. Elsewhere old-fashioned
Clothes hang among cobwebs. Also another
Chamber contains certain beauties asleep, to be woken
Never, and that is myself alongside them.
Returning to green light, coming out into sunlight
Or into rain, that is better, under twinkle or falling
Of leaves. Not thinking too much; if I can,
Continuing aware, in my shreds of being, under
Leaves twinkling or yellow and falling;
On the low terrace in the old terms saying,
Although you may not listen, ecstasy
And then as well peace be with you.

Autumnal

From that slight dell Echo was first
    The voice of elves.
Then, in that temenos, among the quinces
And the roses, it seemed we could
    Forget our selves;

Who are always exiled, never
    Permitted to return,
To invisibles advancing, watching
The latest stubbles of the reaped
    Time lazily burn.

Downland Thoughts about a Poetry
Occasion

Now a grey sky does the whole world house
Have they floored part of the Poets' Corner
With your name; I hear, next to Browning's
Stone; which is a cold fame, Gerard;

Who maimed your own great self; and worse,
Whose self was maimed by supercilious
Thin priests by whom, from pulpits even,
Now you are proclaimed, and claimed;

Who set with cold indifference your name
On the cold stem of a wheel-cross,
In a foreign cemetery, in a list of
Sparrow-names, O rarest Gerard, who knew and who

Declared how, under this grey housing
Pressing down, does the great sun break
Through, and suddenly, as now,
Does all our cold wide earth enflame.